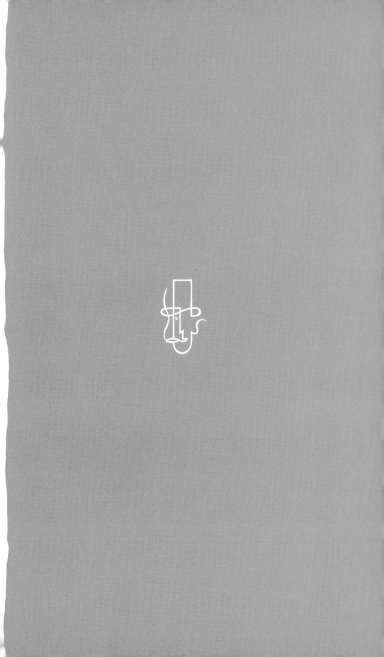

The Art of Fine Cigars

BY JOHN-MANUEL ANDRIOTE,
ANDREW E. FALK, AND B. HENRY PÉREZ

PHOTOGRAPHY BY JAMES V. GLEASON

A Bulfinch Press Book

LITTLE, BROWN AND COMPANY

Boston   New York   Toronto   London

For Jerri, Bud, Laura Goldstein, Manuel Padrón,
our families and friends

First Edition

ISBN 0-8212-2349-6

Library of Congress Catalog Card Number 96-76816

Produced by Elliott & Clark Publishing
Designed by Gibson Parsons Design
Text by John-Manuel Andriote, Andrew E. Falk, and B. Henry Pérez
Edited by Diane Furtney
Photography © 1996 as attributed on page 112

Special thanks to Georgetown Tobacco, a shop in Washington, D.C.,
and Blue-N-Gold, a microbrewery/cigar bar/restaurant in Arlington,
Virginia, for graciously allowing photography on their premises.

Bulfinch Press is an imprint and trademark of Little, Brown and Company (Inc.)
Published simultaneously in Canada by Little, Brown & Company (Canada) Ltd.

PRINTED IN HONG KONG

Contents

Preface

Surely Sigmund Freud was right when he said that, notwithstanding the psychological symbolism he associated with the male body part it resembles, sometimes a cigar *is* just a cigar. Even Freud—great cigar aficionado that he was—knew that it is hard to speak of a cigar as "just" anything. That's because fine cigars represent so many things, all literally rolled into one seemingly straightforward tube shape. Not only are they natural products derived from the earth's bounty, they are products—like fine wines or single-malt Scotches—that capture in their taste and aroma the unique qualities of the soil, water, and sunlight of the particular place on earth—*terroir*, as the French put it—where their ingredients originated. They embody a history and culture, and result from centuries-old styles of manufacture. Perhaps more than anything, cigars provide a vehicle by which to escape, however briefly, to a place in the mind and heart where relaxation,

"SOMETIMES A CIGAR IS JUST A CIGAR."

reflection, and sensuous pleasure combine to make a special time apart.

Our personal experiences as cigar smokers are emblematic of the reasons why cigars are enjoying a renaissance, particularly among people in our own late twenties to thirties age group. Andrew Falk remembers fondly the warm summer evenings spent relaxing with a cigar as he sat on the dock at his parents' home in Annapolis, Maryland. Too young at that point to legally enter the town's bars, Andrew and his friends would sit for hours at the water's edge and enjoy their cigars and one another's company. Small wonder that a mutual appreciation of cigars and other fine organic products became a key part of the friendship that Andrew and Henry Pérez began as undergrads at Georgetown University. For Henry, cigars offered a way to connect to his family's past in their ancestral Cuba. There in the cigar's homeland, Henry's great-grandfather, who emigrated from the Canary Islands to Cuba as a boy in the late nineteenth century, was never without his briefcase that contained a *chaveta* and tobacco leaf he had grown himself so he could roll his own cigars. For his part, John-Manuel Andriote recalls with chagrin his own first cigar: after a dinner with his college roommates on Boston's Beacon Hill to celebrate his twenty-first birthday, he inhaled for the first and only time. Older and wiser, John now puffs his occasional cigar with a bit more panache and considerably less coughing.

However you come to be a smoker of fine cigars, one thing is clear: the more you know about where cigars come from, how they are made, how to smoke them properly, and how they fit with other finer things in life, the greater your enjoyment will be. Whether it's cigars or wine or classical music, your appreciation of artistry and your pleasure increase proportionally to your knowledge of what goes into their composition. There may be times when a cigar is just a cigar, but that cigar can be all you need to open your mind and senses to new vistas of pleasurable experience you might not otherwise know.

This book is not a definitive encyclopedia of cigar brands. It doesn't assume that you know a great deal about cigars already. It won't overwhelm and intimidate you with pretense and arcana. What you have in your hand is simply a primer, a friendly and informative guide to the essentials involved in the history, manufacture, smoking, and storage of fine cigars. Our goal is simply to share our own enjoyment of fine cigars with you and to equip you with all you need to know to appreciate the art of fine cigars.

Orientation:
Time and Place

Whether or not you believe that Columbus discovered the New World, one thing is certain: he was the first European to bring tobacco back to the Old World. After finding a safe bay in which to anchor his ships, Columbus sent two men to explore the interior of the island we know today as Cuba. The two, Luis de Torres and Rodrigo de Xérez, returned a few days later with tales of a bizarre thing they had seen. Arriving at a small collection of palm huts, they had encountered a group of natives sucking on a "musket" made of burning leaves that emitted a fragrant gray smoke— apparently a religious rite. They were intrigued; so intrigued, in fact, that upon their return to Spain, Rodrigo was caught indulging in his new habit by officials of the Inquisition and was imprisoned for demonic practices. You can imagine his surprise years later when, released from prison, he found that the townspeople had adopted his habit.

New world natives are depicted harvesting and smoking tobacco in this French print from 1557.

The use of tobacco spread throughout Europe. By the end of the sixteenth century, tobacco had been introduced to Germany through gifts from the conquistadors to Holy Roman Emperor Charles V. The French ambassador to Portugal, Jean Nicot, sent packages of tobacco to his queen—Catherine de Médicis, wife of Henri II of France—who ingested it in powdered form as what she believed to be a cure-all. Besides giving tobacco to France, Nicot was so identified with the introduction of tobacco to Europe that nicotine and the Latin name for tobacco, *Nicotiana tabacum*, forever linked him with the leaf. Sir Walter Raleigh, besides writing poetry, also enjoyed a good smoke, and in fact was one of the first men to introduce tobacco to England.

DEMAND INCREASES FOR THE GOLDEN LEAF

By the seventeenth century, tobacco smoking had become so popular in Europe that paintings by Dutch Old Masters often depicted men smoking pipes. Spanish treasure ships returning from the New World were laden with gold, silver, and the "golden leaf," tobacco, to feed the increasing demand of Europeans. By 1636, the Spanish Crown organized Tabacalera as a monopoly to handle the export and processing of tobacco. In those days, the monopoly was rented out to the private sector.

As demand continued to increase in the eighteenth century, Cuba and other Caribbean islands developed plantations, or *vegas*, where tobacco competed with cattle and sugar to become Cuba's major agricultural industry. At this point Europe's upper classes were taking their tobacco in the form of snuff—tobacco ground to a powder and snorted through the nostrils. In fact, European monarchs were so enamored of snuff that they commissioned the finest jewelers to create ornate, diamond-encrusted snuff boxes. The Prussian king,

Frederick the Great, owned one of Europe's finest collections of such boxes and could often be found in the gilded salons of Sans Souci opening his treasured boxes to partake of the pleasures of the golden leaf.

Gentlemen are portrayed sampling tobacco in this eighteenth-century woodcut attributed to Thomas Bewick.

THE MODERN CIGAR DEBUTS IN SEVILLE

It wasn't until the end of the eighteenth century that cigars as we know them first became popular outside Spain. Spain had conquered the Caribbean in the sixteenth century, and Cuban tobacco was being shipped in bulk to the port city of Seville. There, beginning in 1717, the leaves were processed and rolled into cigars. It was also in Seville that what we think of as the modern cigar—consisting of filler, binder, and a wrapper—originated. During England's brief occupation of Cuba in 1763, English sailors brought back what were probably the first cigars to reach England. But it was not until Napoléon and Wellington's troops returned home with cigars after the Peninsular War in Spain (1808–1812) that cigars were brought to the attention of the French, English, and other Europeans. Cigars became the fashionable way for the upper classes to "take" tobacco. Wealthy Englishmen thought cigars more refined than pipes; given their higher cost, cigars offered the elite yet another way to proclaim social and economic superiority. In 1820 the English set up their first cigar factory, followed the next year by Parliament's establishment of industry regulations.

Naturally, the increased demand for high-quality cigars in Europe was a boon for

The Partagás Fabrica in Havana, Cuba.

Spain, which began colonial rule in Cuba in 1511. Like many colonies, Cuba supplied only raw products to its ruling country. But as the colonial relationship between Spain and Cuba evolved over two centuries, the colony began to develop its own local processing industry. In the early 1700s the colony was granted permission by the Spanish crown to develop mills to process tobacco—the first sign of Cuba's economic independence.

The second would come in the early 1800s. King Ferdinand VII issued a decree in 1821 allowing Cuba to make cigars and export them to Spain rather than sending raw tobacco for Spanish manufacture. In appreciation of Ferdinand, Cuba each year presents to the King of Spain a box of the highest-quality Cuban cigars—the mythic Trinidad cigars.

In the early nineteenth century the renowned Cuban cigar firm, Partagás, founded by Jaime Partagás in 1827, began purchasing plantations in the Vuelta Abajo and Semi Vuelta regions of Cuba. In 1845 Partagás built its famous factory in Havana that to this day remains a monument to the cigar industry. By the mid-1800s there were 9,500 tobacco plantations and as many as 1,300 cigar factories in Cuba. Cigar making had reached great heights in Cuba and was now a full-fledged industry. Because of this proliferation of manufacturers, cigar makers began to use boxes and bands as well as size and shape differences to distinguish their products from one another.

UNCLE SAM TAKES UP CIGAR SMOKING

Cigar smoking didn't become popular in America until the Civil War, although the nation's first cigar factory opened in 1810 in Hartford, Connecticut, and President John Quincy Adams (who served 1825–1829) was a devotee of fine cigars. Conestoga, Pennsylvania, produced some of America's best-known cigars, including the long stogie named after the town. In Key West, Florida, a thriving cigar industry during this period was bolstered by the expertise of Cubans who had fled colonial rule. But it wasn't until the 1920s that a cheap cigar would be mass-produced by machines and catch fire, so to speak, among the less well-heeled—who no doubt agreed with Woodrow Wilson's vice president, Thomas

Cigars were popular among officers and enlisted men during the Civil War.

Marshall, when he told the U.S. Senate in 1919, "What this country really needs is a good five-cent cigar."

THE POLITICS OF CIGAR MAKING

As the Cuban cigar industry grew during colonial times, those who worked in the industry helped found the colony's industrial working class. In both the nineteenth and twentieth centuries, the *fabricas de tabacos*—factories where cigars were made—became centers of political agitation. When Cuba struggled to be free of its four-hundred-year domination by Spain in the 1890s war of independence, a number of cigar makers fled the island for other Caribbean islands or the United States. José Marti, the revered Cuban patriot and avid cigar smoker, called on his Cuban countrymen to rise up against Spanish rule in a note he sent to Cuba inside a cigar dispatched from his exile in Key West. After Cuba won its independence, cigar workers continued to be politically active. In fact, in the 1930s, the owners of Partagás closed their Havana factory for a short time during labor unrest. When Fidel Castro overthrew the Cuban government in 1959, he began to nationalize the country's major industries, including its cigar works. The government took control of cigar houses and large tobacco plantations in 1960, when Castro formed a state cigar company called Cubatabaco (today called Habanos, S.A.). Ramon Cifuentes, whose family had owned Partagás since 1900, recalls in *Cigar Aficionado* (Winter 1995-96) how he had been at the factory in September 1960 and had been told to leave the premises immediately, without being able to remove anything from his offices. He was told by authorities that his business had been "interned."

Even after nationalization, most tobacco farms were still privately owned, but Castro limited the size of privately held *vegas* to five to ten acres. Farmers today cannot own more than fifteen acres. Before the revolution, farmers would sell their crops to brokers who then sold the tobacco to cigar houses such as Partagás, the producers of Montecristo. Now they are allowed to sell their crops only to the government and at a price determined by the government at harvest time.

Since the United States imposed an embargo on Cuba in July 1963, Cuban cigars can't be imported legally into the States. Under the Trading with the Enemy Act, as applied to Cuba, U.S. citizens can't purchase products of Cuban origin and import them into the United States, whether in Cuba or in a third

"WHAT THIS COUNTRY REALLY NEEDS IS A GOOD FIVE-CENT CIGAR."

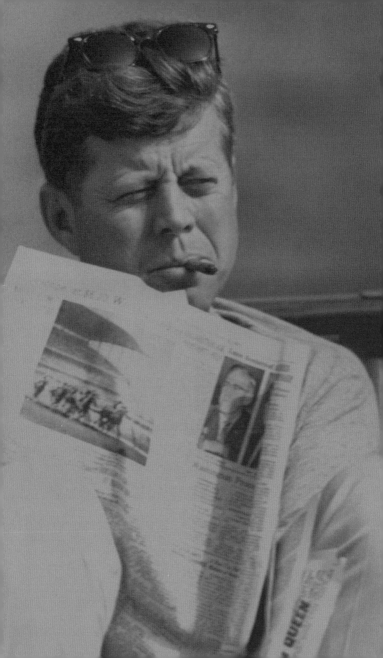

country, and are subject to fines and imprisonment if they do. On a note of irony, the story is told that the night before President John F. Kennedy authorized the Cuban embargo, he arranged to have a large cache of Cuban cigars delivered for his personal use. At Kennedy's request, his press secretary Pierre Salinger procured overnight 1,200 Petit Upmanns—the president's favorite. Immediately upon receiving the cigars, Kennedy pulled from his desk drawer and signed the legislation banning Cuban products. Perhaps Kennedy's treasured cigars were stored in his humidor that sold at auction at Sotheby's in April 1996 to *Cigar Aficionado* publisher Marvin Shanken for $574,000.

Fortunately for U.S. citizens, many of Cuba's major cigar-factory owners—like their countrymen in the late nineteenth century—fled the Communist regime and set up shop elsewhere. Famous names such as Cifuentes, H. Upmann, Romeo y Julieta, and Hoyo de Monterrey can still be found, though the cigars now are made of non-Cuban tobacco and are from other parts of

President Kennedy is pictured here in the late summer of 1963, as he partakes of a cigar and a newspaper shipboard off Cape Cod.

the Caribbean, including the Dominican Republic, Jamaica, the Canary Islands, Honduras, and Mexico. We'll talk more about brands and this potentially confusing duplication of brand names in the chapter "Selection and Storage."

By the time many of us discovered fine handmade cigars (as well as gourmet coffees and single-malt Scotches) in the mid-1990s, the cigar industry had been in a slump for years. Cigar consumption had been in decline since the 1960s. That has changed drastically. In 1995, Americans bought 163 million premium cigars according to the Cigar Association of America—up from 97 million just four years earlier. At the end of 1995, the *New York Times* described some of the people who have come to enjoy fine cigars in the past few years. The reporter said of the men she observed enjoying a smoke at Manhattan's Cigar Bar (at Beekman Bar and Books, on First Avenue at Fiftieth Street) "The new cigar smokers have little in common with the stereotypical stogie-chomping truck drivers and fat-cat politicians of old. This new wave tends to be young (mid twenties to late thirties), better educated, and very discriminating as to what cigars are smoked and where."

Here at the end of the century, we cigar lovers would seem to be fulfilling a kind of historic destiny to take the love of cigars—and ensure the survival of their manufacture—into the next millennium.

LOCATION, LOCATION, LOCATION: WHERE DO CIGARS COME FROM?

Cigars are agricultural products. But unlike, say, corn or soybeans, the tobacco that goes into making fine cigars is grown success-fully—exquisitely—only in certain areas of the world. The French speak of *terroir*, a word that can't easily be translated but that in English is what we so artlessly call microcli-mate. Only specific, circumscribed areas have the unique combination of soil, rainfall, temperature, humidity, and sunlight needed to produce the high-quality tobacco used in fine cigars. Burgundy, of course, is home to many of the world's finest red wines made from the pinot noir grape, but Burgundy's soil and climate are not conducive to tobacco growing. Likewise the areas of the world—chiefly in and around the Caribbean—that grow outstanding tobacco wouldn't be hospi-table to the pinot noir, nor any other wine grape for that matter. Just as a particular wine can speak of a place as specific as the $4\frac{1}{3}$-acre slope that makes up the vineyard Romanée-Conti in Burgundy, or Napanook in Napa

A FINE CIGAR IS A KIND OF EARTH PRINT OF ITS LAND OF ORIGIN.

Valley, so too a fine cigar is a kind of earth print of its land of origin.

FIRST OF ALL, CUBA

Of course Cuba, which perfected the art of fine cigars as we know them, is legendary for its tobacco. The five main tobacco-growing areas in Cuba are Vuelta Abajo, Semi Vuelta, Partido, Remedios, and Oriente, which includes the Vuelta Arriba. Tobacco grown in Pinar del Rio, the westernmost region of Cuba, is generally considered the best in the world. The lush, green area, with its climate, rainfall, and reddish sandy loam are ideal for tobacco growth. Small wonder that tobacco production is the region's leading industry. The Vuelta Abajo occupies most of Pinar del Rio,

and it is here that about 2,500 acres are devoted to wrapper leaf and 5,000 acres to binders—hardly enormous tracts of land given the worldwide demand for these leaves. It is in this region that one finds the tropical, much-photographed Valle Viñales. The sixty-five-inch average annual rainfall in Pinar del Rio is one of Cuba's highest. In one of the quirks of nature that makes this region the prime area for tobacco that it is, the rainfall drops significantly during the growing season, November to February. Even in these dry months, however, there is a danger that a storm will severely damage the tobacco crop. During these crucial months the average temperature is eighty degrees Fahrenheit with sixty-four percent humidity.

Other areas of Cuba where tobacco is grown include the Partidos area near Havana, where high-quality wrappers are grown. There is also Remedios, in the center of the island, and Oriente at the island's eastern end, both of which produce tobacco, though of a lesser grade than in Pinar del Rio. Tobacco from these two areas is often used for making the *tripa* (literally "guts"), or filler, of cigars.

THE DOMINICAN REPUBLIC SURGES FORWARD

The Dominican Republic, east of Cuba, shares a similar climate, especially in the Cibao river valley, where most of the country's tobacco is grown. Since the Cuban revolution and the 1963 American ban on the importation of Cuban products

to the United States, the Dominican Republic has risen to become the leading supplier of
high-quality handmade cigars sold in the U.S.

The Dominican Re-
public has seen its cigar
sales skyrocket in the
past few years, to the
point that this tiny
nation that shares an
island with Haiti now
supplies more than half
the handmade cigars imported into the
United States. In 1995 the United States
imported 81.1 million cigars from the Dominican Republic, over 30 million more cigars
than Cuba produced altogether in the same
year. One of the most important reasons why
the Dominican Republic has made its rise is
that a number of Cuba's major cigar brands
(such as Partagás) moved their production
from Cuba to the Dominican Republic when
Castro nationalized Cuba's cigar industry.
Most tobacco grown in the Dominican
Republic is for filler and binder. It imports
wrappers from Connecticut (more on the

Constitution state to follow), Cameroon, Brazil, Honduras, Mexico, and Ecuador. Cigars from the Dominican Republic are generally milder and lighter than those produced in either Cuba or Honduras.

HONDURAS BENEFITS FROM CUBAN EXILES

Honduras was one of the first places where Cuban cigar makers relocated when Castro nationalized the cigar industry. Cuban tobacco seed allegedly was smuggled into Honduras shortly after Castro's rise to power, and that seed continues to provide much of the country's filler and binder plantings even today. Unfortunately, Cuban seed plants are

unusually susceptible to blue mold disease, a fungus that can decimate an entire field of tobacco in days. Because of the preponderance of Cuban seed in Honduras, blue mold disease has been savage, and in the early 1980s it decimated much of the Honduran crop.

Honduran cigars are widely considered to be the closest to Cuban cigars in style and flavor, which typically means they are big, strong cigars with a lot of depth and flavor.

Honduras was the beneficiary of the legendary Zino Davidoff's affection and attention. A longtime presence in Cuba and world-renowned champion of fine cigars and fine living, Davidoff started a line of cigars, called the Zino, in Honduras while he continued to produce his famous cigars in Havana. But in 1990, following a reputed dispute with Cubatabaco, Davidoff closed his Cuban production and moved to the Dominican Republic. He believed that country to have the most potential to produce high-quality cigars outside of Cuba.

AS FOR THE REST OF THE CIGAR-MAKING WORLD

Other countries in the Caribbean and Central America with notable cigar industries include Jamaica, Mexico, and Nicaragua. On the other side of the world, the Indonesian islands of Java and Sumatra have long had links to cigar manufacturers in Germany, the Netherlands, and Switzerland, as has the Philippines with Spain.

Some of the world's best wrapper leaf is produced, surprisingly enough, in Connecticut. Of course, the New England state hardly has the subtropical climate of the Caribbean islands. But top-quality cigar tobacco—including its famous wrapper—is grown under 10-foot-high gauze tents that are used to shield the leaves from the harsh rays of the sun (hence the wrapper name, "Connecticut Shade"). The growing and curing process is expensive, so typically a cigar with a Connecticut Shade wrapper will increase the cost by an additional 50 cents to a dollar.

As with real estate, location is everything when you talk about the growing of tobacco and the making of fine cigars. Variations in the soil, sun, rainfall, and humidity account for the variations in taste and aroma of the cigars you purchase at your local tobacconist. What begins its life in the rarified atmosphere of an equatorial island makes its way to you by way of a great deal of care and attention. When you light up your cigar, then, you are literally partaking of a fruit of the earth as well as the fruit of a great deal of labor. With that in mind, let's look next at what, exactly, that fruit and labor comprise.

From Leaf to Puro: The Making of a Fine Cigar

I n order to truly appreciate the *art* of fine cigars—or *puros*, as they are often referred to in Spanish-speaking countries because they consist entirely of tobacco—it is useful to know something of the *science* of growing and processing the tobacco that goes into them. And, of course, the actual making of cigars is both a science and an art, so we'll also look at the centuries-old craft of making cigars by hand.

Tending eight-week-old tobacco plants at El Cojoro wrapper plantation, near San Juan y Martínez, Cuba.

GROWING TOBACCO

As we have noted, cigars are agricultural products. Long before a cigar becomes a cigar, the tobacco that goes into it begins as a seed. Tobacco seeds are planted in flat beds and covered with straw or cloth to shade them. About thirty-five days after the tobacco seed germinates, it is transplanted to a field where it is watered by rain, morning dew, and

subterranean irrigation. The plants grow rapidly and soon develop buds that must be removed by hand—in a process called *desbotonar*, or unbuttoning—so the plant will concentrate on leaf production and not divert energy to producing flowers. If you've ever grown the variegated coleus or aromatic basil, you will understand this process of debudding for the sake of producing lusher foliage. After a labor-intensive 120 days or so—during which the plants may be tended as many as 170 times—the seedlings have matured into full-grown tobacco plants ready for harvest.

DESBOTONAR: DEBUDDING FOR THE SAKE OF PRODUCING LUSHER FOLIAGE.

ANATOMY OF A TOBACCO PLANT

Let's look at the parts of the tobacco plant so you can see where they factor into the finished cigar. There are three main parts of the plant: the top (*corona* and *semi-corona*,), the middle (*centro gordo*, *centro fino*, and *centro ligero*), and bottom (*uno y medio* and *libra de pie*). Altogether a tobacco plant generally has sixteen or seventeen leaves. The tobacco is harvested from the bottom up in six phases, each a week apart. First, the *libra de pie*, then the *uno y medio, centro ligero, centro fino, centro gordo*, and finally the *corona*. The leaves in the top section are referred to as the *ligero* leaves. Because of their greater exposure to the sun, the *ligero* leaves are oily and have a stronger flavor, so they are used for binder or filler. The best leaves are found in the plant's midsection, and they are referred to as the *seco* leaves. The *seco* leaves are lighter and are used for either wrapper or filler. Leaves at the base of the plant, the *volado* leaves, are generally used for filler because they burn well.

Corona

Semi-corona

Centro Gordo

Centro Fino

Centro Ligero

Uno Y Medio

Libra De Pie

CURING THE TOBACCO

After harvest, the tobacco leaves are bundled and transported to nearby tobacco barns—the barns face east and west so the sun heats them in the morning and afternoon—for aging and curing. About a hundred leaves are strung with needle and thread onto wooden poles (*cujes*) that are hoisted high inside the barn, where air circulates around them for the next forty-five to sixty days. After they are dried and have turned from green to brown, the leaves are carefully removed from the *cujes* and stacked into bundles according to type. In Cuba today, most plantations in the Pinar del Rio region perform only this first step in processing cigar tobacco, after which the state monopoly moves the tobacco from the drying barns to central warehouses in the Vuelta Abajo region.

Wrapper leaves hung in a curing barn, La Guira, Cuba.

The next phase involves two fermentations of the tobacco. The fermentation process makes the tobacco used in cigars less acidic and lower in tar and nicotine than that used in cigarettes. This is one of the reasons why cigars taste smoother than cigarettes and don't burn as hot. Another reason is that throughout the aging process of the tobacco, people are constantly sorting and selecting the leaves, ensuring that only the best are used in fine cigars. Cigarettes generally are made of inferior grades of tobacco that haven't been cured as extensively as cigar tobacco. Like machine-made cigars, which we advise you to avoid, cigarettes also use portions of tobacco leaf rather than whole leaves.

From the drying barns the leaves go to the fermentation houses, where they are placed in three-foot piles and covered with burlap. Moisture in the leaves triggers the fermentation process—similar to composting—and by the end of another thirty-five to forty days the leaves will have assumed a uniform brown color. From the fermentation house the leaves are placed in large square boxes lined with palm leaves, then transported to the sorting house, or *escogida*, where they are graded by color, size, and texture. After being flattened, the filler leaves have part of their stems and veins stripped out in a delicate operation. To make handling them easier the leaves are moistened, either with water for the fine wrappers or a murky cocktail of water and tobacco-stem juice for the fillers. Each leaf is sorted and graded. Broken leaves are relegated to cigarettes or filler for machine-made cigars.

A second fermentation begins after the moistened, sorted, and graded leaves are piled in six-foot stacks (*burros*) in dark rooms. In the center of each *burro* is a wooden casing. A thermometer inserted into the casing monitors the temperature at the center of the stack for the next two months. If the temperature exceeds 110° F, the stack is broken down and rebuilt to allow equal time for fermentation of the leaves on the outside. After this second fermentation the leaves are flattened again and baled into square units called *tercios*. At long last, the tobacco is ready for the cigar factory. But once there, the tobacco may continue to age in a warehouse for as long as two years, kept the whole time at the ideal temperature and humidity. Some cigars, such as the famous Cohiba cigars made in Cuba, go through yet another fermentation after they arrive at the factory from the warehouse.

As you can see, before the tobacco is considered ready for use in a fine cigar, it has already attained a place among the earth's most tenderly nurtured and fussed-over agricultural products. You can better appreciate the cost of finished cigars when you understand that the making of a fine cigar is both a capital- and labor-intensive operation. And you begin to see the reasons why cigars are so

THE WRAPPER LEAF IS THE MOST DELICATE COMPONENT OF THE CIGAR.

often spoken of in the same conversations as fine wines, cognacs, single malts, and other pleasurable products resulting from years of hard work and tender care.

IT'S A WRAP

Let's look a bit more closely at the cigar wrapper. It's the first thing you notice in a cigar, and its aesthetic appeal—in addition to its flavor and burning qualities—is an important aspect of the finished product. Because the wrapper leaf is the most delicate

Rolling a Montecristo at H. Upmann, Havana, Cuba.

component of the cigar, it is harvested from special tobacco plants that are grown under gauze sheets to protect them against the sun (recall the description of Connecticut Shade wrapper in the previous chapter). This technique, known as *tapado* (covering), prevents the leaves from becoming too thick and helps them stay smooth, delicate, and less blemished by large veins. Unblemished wrapper leaves from one plant will provide enough wrapper for as many as thirty-two cigars. Because the wrapper leaf is the most crucial and delicate component of a cigar, it is the pampered child of the *vega*, the tobacco plantation. It can take upwards of three years to obtain a high-quality wrapper, including the year-long growing period, then six months to process and another eighteen months for aging. The ideal wrapper leaf must be at least fifteen inches long and four inches wide. Producing such a delicate product is expensive; a great wrapper leaf, whether it is grown in Connecticut, Cuba, or Cameroon, adds significantly to a cigar's cost.

A MATTER OF CLASS

Wrapper leaves that are grown under tents are classified by color, from green to light brown, with as many as sixty-five shades in between. The many shades of wrapper leaves are classified within three categories to at least eighteen grades based on size, color, and texture. Great skill is needed in sorting through the subtle differences in each wrapper leaf. Growers pick the wrapper leaves two or three at a time, passing over the fields on six separate occasions. This process resembles the picking of *botrytised* grapes (grapes that have been affected by the "Noble Rot," *Botrytis cinerea*) for making the prized Sauternes wines at Château d'Yquem, where pickers select grapes one by one over the course of several passes through the vineyards, looking for perfect ripeness in each grape.

Of Cuba's 100,000 acres currently planted with tobacco, only one-fifth is dedicated to growing wrapper leaf. Cuban wrapper is a rich dark brown compared to the lighter brown or even yellowish tones of Connecticut Shade. If the Vuelta Abajo area of Cuba is the Côte d'Or of the cigar world, then the Corojo plantation can be compared to the Domaine de la Romanée-Conti. Without a doubt the Corojo plantation is the world's greatest *vega* for shade-grown tobacco. The state-owned 395-acre plantation, located between the towns of San Luis y Martínez and San Juan, in the heart of the Vuelta Abajo, has a combination of soil and unique tobacco plant that makes its wrapper leaf the finest grown in Cuba and one of the most prized in the world. In pre-Castro Cuba, El Corojo supplied wrapper to the esteemed cigar maker Upmann for use in Montecristo cigars. El Corojo's unusual and exceptional wrapper is the result of the efforts of Diego Menéndez, who ran the *vega* in the 1930s and 1940s and who developed

UNBLEMISHED WRAPPER LEAVES FROM ONE PLANT WILL PROVIDE ENOUGH WRAPPER FOR AS MANY AS THIRTY-TWO CIGARS.

"The World's Best Wrapper," as *Cigar Aficionado* calls it (Summer 1995). Menéndez's granddaughter, Adelaida Pérez Fuentes, told the magazine that the *corojo*, named for the plantation, is a "genetically distinct plant," with unique color, texture, and size.

The Dominican Republic traditionally produced no wrapper leaf of its own, importing all its wrappers from Connecticut, Ecuador, Nicaragua, Brazil, and Cameroon (wrapper from Cameroon, produced jointly with the Central African Republic, is noticeably dark, rich, oily, textured by bumps, and preferred by Europeans). But recently, some manufacturers in the Dominican Republic— most notably, Arturo Fuente, Inc.—have had success growing shade wrapper. Honduran cigars predominantly use Connecticut seed wrapper.

We will talk about the current shortage of wrapper leaf in the final chapter. Now, though, let's look at how fermented and aged tobacco goes from its raw form to the perfect cigar you can buy from a tobacconist many, many miles from its place of origin.

A worker bunches a cigar in a gallery at the Partagás Fabrica, Havana, Cuba.

HOW CIGARS ARE MADE

Fine cigars—handmade, that is—are the end product of a craft that is equal parts art and science. As any cigar roller, or *tabaquero*, will tell you, the work that goes into making fine cigars includes a good deal of love and devotion. Consider the words of Amparo Jiménez, a 56-year-old Cuban expatriate working as a *tabaquero* in Miami for Ernesto Pérez Carillo, the Cuban-American owner of El Credito, which produces several different cigar brands including the famous La Gloria Cubana. In a 1995 *Washington Post* article, Jiménez says, "This is manual work, and I like everything about it. You must have art and love for it…. It takes a lot of effort to make the product the best it can be, with good flavor, an even burn, and a smooth draw…. I'm here because I make people happy with what I do."

INSIDE THE *FABRICA*

And what Jiménez does, like thousands of *tabaqueros* at work today and for centuries since cigars were first made, is indeed pains-

A STAR ROLLER CAN MAKE 150 CIGARS A DAY.

taking work. Rollers work in large rooms, or galleries, governed by rules and customs dating from the nineteenth century. In the gallery are dozens, perhaps even hundreds, of rollers, about half of them men, half women. A Cuban *tabaquero* traditionally would spend as long as two years as an apprentice, observing and absorbing the steps and culture of the *tabaqueria* before being allowed to roll a cigar. Even then they would be permitted to roll only the smaller-sized ones. In Cuba, rollers are graded on a scale of four to seven, with grade seven reserved for only the best rollers. These star rollers are responsible for making the most difficult cigars, often the largest or most uniquely shaped, the *figurados*.

One reason why Cuba's cigar makers became politically aware in the nineteenth century was because they were well-informed about current events and politics: as they worked the rollers would listen to a *lector*—generally one of the rollers selected by the others for his eloquence—read aloud from newspapers and books while the rollers worked. Because rollers are paid according to the number of cigars they produce, the *lector* was compensated for the time he was not actually making cigars by contributions from other rollers. The name of what became Cuba's leading cigar brand, Montecristo, resulted from this tradition. In the nineteenth century, the works of Dumas were the most popular books read by the *lectors* to the rollers. Their absolute favorite was *The Count*

of Monte Cristo. In homage to Dumas and his count, the Montecristo label was created in the 1930s.

A good cigar roller can make about 100 medium-sized cigars per day. A highly skilled, star roller may make as many as 150 a day—averaging one cigar every four to five minutes. Despite the training and skill it takes to be a cigar roller, the work is not highly compensated. At Miami's El Credito even the best *tabaqueros* earn only $20,000–25,000 a year. In Cuba they earn roughly 350–400 pesos a month (the equivalent of $14 to $16)—plus five cigars a day. While this sum may seem small, it is more than double the average monthly income in Cuba.

CIGAR PARTS

There are three parts of the handmade cigar: filler, binder, and wrapper. Because the outer wrapper, or *capa*, largely determines the cigar's appearance and aroma, it is made from selected leaves fermented separately so that they are soft and not too oily. The leaves can't have protruding veins and must be pliable enough that the roller can handle them easily. The binder leaf, the *capote* (as in Truman), literally binds the cigar's insides. It usually comes from the top part of the plant, where its exposure to the sun gives it a coarseness and strength to hold the cigar together. At the cigar's core is the filler. Three types of filler leaves are folded lengthwise by hand to allow smoke to be drawn through when the cigar is

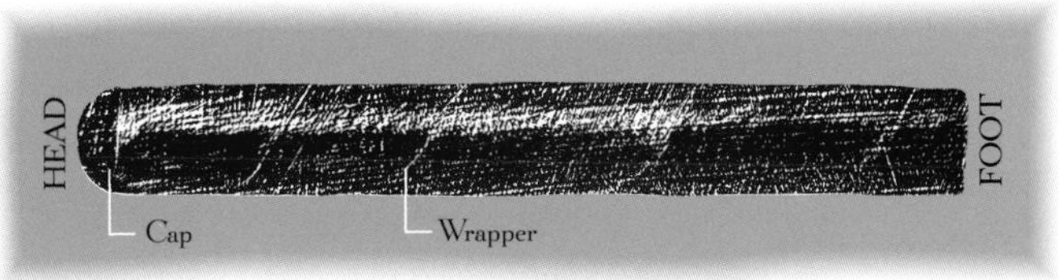

HEAD

FOOT

Cap

Wrapper

lit. Oily and long-burning *ligero* leaves, from the top of the plant, are placed in the center of the cigar to make it burn slowly. Lighter *seco* leaves, from the middle of the plant, are used next. Finally, the relatively flavorless *volado* leaves, from the bottom of the plant, are added because they burn well.

The blending of these different leaves in the filler contributes significantly to the distinctive flavor of the various sizes and brands of cigars. A stronger cigar will have a higher proportion of *ligero* in its filler, whereas a lighter cigar will have more *seco* and *volado*. As with the blending of single malts from various harvests and distilleries to achieve a blended Scotch whisky, the blending of tobacco leaves in the filler is determined by the desired cigar flavor. Tobacco from two different regions can be used, as well as tobacco from different years. Certain cigar brands may use a particular blend of filler to arrive at a "house style"—their own recipe, so to speak—so that each of their cigar types has a consistent taste year after year. The size and ring gauge of a cigar also affect its taste.

LIKE THOSE WHO BLEND SCOTCH, CIGAR MAKERS HAVE THEIR OWN "HOUSE STYLE."

After the wrapper, binder, and filler have been selected, the wrapper leaf is gently flattened and stretched in an upside-down position so that its veins face inside the cigar. Two to four filler leaves are laid end to end and rolled into the binder leaves. This is called the "bunch." The bunch is then pressed into a wooden mold to set. The resulting cylindrical bunch is laid onto the wrapper at an angle. Then the wrapper leaf is wound, stretched around the bunch, and glued with a flavorless vegetable gum. The cigar is rolled with a steel blade called a *chaveta*. A small, rounded piece of wrapper is used to form the cap, which is added to prevent the cigar from unraveling. Some of the best cigars are capped using the flag method, in which the cigar is closed by twisting the end of the wrapper rather than by adding a separate cap. The open end is cut to the desired length.

FINISHED CIGARS

The cigar is now complete. At this point, Henry's great-grandfather would take great joy in smoking the freshly rolled cigar, which is much stronger than an aged cigar and is enjoyed by many Cubans. But the cigar makers are attentive to the tastes of European customers, who prefer the rounder, less sharp taste of an aged cigar. For this reason most cigar factories store the cigars in temperature-controlled cabinets for three weeks. Each cabinet holds about 18,000 cigars.

This finishes their fermentation and allows excess moisture to evaporate.

Professional smokers sample a certain percentage of each roller's finished cigars—grading them according to criteria including length, weight, firmness, the wrapper's smoothness, and how well the ends are cut. Others will grade the cigars according to aroma and how well they burn and draw. In batches of one thousand from a particular brand and size, the cigars are sent in wooden boxes for a final grading according to color. The color grader sorts the cigars to ensure that all cigars in a box are the same color. After color grading, the cigars are sent to the packing department, where the bands are put on. Then it's into the Spanish cedar boxes in which you ultimately see them. Even as they are being packed, the cigars are examined for any flaws that may have escaped the rigorous quality-control processes.

By the time the cigars reach your local tobacconist, they have been scrutinized more closely and more often than most products made by human hands. But the cigar's con-

BY THE TIME CIGARS REACH YOUR LOCAL TONACCONIST, THEY HAVE BEEN SCRUTINIZED MORE CLOSELY AND MORE OFTEN THAN MOST PRODUCTS MADE BY HUMAN HANDS.

struction and quality are essential to your enjoyment of it. It takes a great deal of skill to make a cigar because, for example, too much filler will make the draw too difficult, while too little filler will make the cigar get hot and burn too fast. It has to be just right. And consistent. Emerson says that a "foolish consistency is the hobgoblin of little minds," but he was referring to self-reliance, obviously not to the knowledge, concentration, and skill it takes to make good cigars consistent.

To make a fine handmade cigar requires more than two hundred steps from the planting and tending of the tobacco seedling to harvest and fermentation to rolling, grading, and packaging. After all the work and care, the finished cigar is ready to make the final leg of its journey from the *vega*, where its tobacco was raised, by way of the cigar factory, to your tobacconist and possibly to your humidor—and into your pleasantest moments. Now that you know how tobacco is grown, cured, and made into a finished cigar, let's look at your options when shopping for fine cigars and how to store them once you bring them home.

Selection and Storage

Okay, you've bought this nifty and informative little book about fine cigars and you're on your way to the tobacco store and the realms of pleasure locked inside ordinary rolled tubes of tobacco. What do you look for, exactly? And how do you decide which tobacconist's shop to patronize? Let's talk a moment about what makes a good tobacconist good.

CHOOSING A TOBACCO SHOP

First of all, you should never feel intimidated going into a tobacco store. Remember, social interaction and good cheer are hallmarks of the pleasure that cigar smokers enjoy. If you walk into a tobacconist's and you feel the sales staff are condescending when you ask questions and admit that you are learning about cigars—leave. Cigar smoking is a hobby and a pleasurable experience. You shouldn't be made to feel there's something flawed in your character simply because you may not know

Deal with a tobacconist who knows the products and enjoys talking about them.

all there is to know about cigars. There are, unfortunately, some shops that are so rigidly formal that even highly knowledgeable aficionados would be loath to do business with them. Andrew remembers the experience of walking into a certain tobacconist's in Man-

hattan, where the sales staff— though they all looked impressive in Italian suits—were so condescending that he was immediately turned off. Shops like that traffic in image and pretense, not in the real reasons why people should smoke cigars, which of course revolve around enjoyment. You should feel comfortable asking about cigars. You should feel that you're dealing with people who know their products and enjoy talking about them. So the first thing to look for is friendly, well-informed staff eager to make you a regular customer.

The next thing is the shop's stock of cigars. Do they have a good selection? How are the cigars stored and displayed? Don't even consider buying a cigar in a shop where boxes of cigars are sitting in the dry, open air. You want to buy cigars in good shape. They should be stored properly in a dedicated space, a humidor. We'll talk more about humidors later in this chapter, but for our purposes here you should know that in a tobacco shop a humidor may be an actual room filled with cigars stored in a temperature- and humidity-controlled space. Or the cigars may be displayed in glass cases that are, again, controlled for heat and moisture. But open boxes of cigars, no matter how artfully displayed, are not to be considered. Don't waste your money or your time in such an inept shop.

SELECTING YOUR CIGARS

If you are the type who needs to be guided by hard and fast rules, you're not a good candidate for becoming a cigar aficionado. If, however, you enjoy sampling life's variety and making up your own mind about what suits you, you're on the right track. Cigar smoking is an imprecise art and its enjoyment a subjective undertaking. Your personal taste will ultimately become the standard against which you measure and evaluate cigars. A good cigar is one that *you* enjoy. No one can dictate your taste. Of course, being exposed to a wide variety of cigars and understanding their respective characteristics are the ways you cultivate your taste. Your taste has become cultivated when you can state not only what you like but also why you like it.

There are several criteria by which to gauge a cigar's suitability to your taste and needs, including the cigar's color, shape, size, and technical quality. After you've had the chance to try a number of different cigars, you're likely to find one brand or several whose qualities suit you. This, of course, is the point of smoking cigars in the first place—and is what this book is intended to help you achieve. Because a cigar's price doesn't necessarily indicate its quality, it will be important to cultivate a sense of a cigar's actual value and evaluate your own tastes. We'll talk more about each of the criteria, but let's begin by looking at the various color categories and what they mean.

COLOR

There can be as many as sixty-five shades of cigar wrapper. For simplicity's sake, cigars are categorized under one of seven fairly encompassing color headings, listed below in order from lightest to darkest:

THE DARKER THE WRAPPER, THE STRONGER AND DEEPER THE CIGAR'S TASTE.

Double claro is a greenish brown color because the leaf is picked before it matures and then is dried rapidly. Because there is little oil in the leaf, the flavor also tends to be on the light side. Double claros used to be popular in the United States, but that has changed as smokers explore the darker, richer color categories.

Claro is light brown, sometimes called natural. Claro is typically the color of Connecticut Shade wrapper. It is used in mild cigars.

Colorado claro, a medium-brown color, is

well-known from Dominican Republic cigars.

Colorado is a maroon shade of dark brown. Colorado-colored cigars are well-matured and aromatic.

Colorado maduro is dark brown, medium in strength, and rich in flavor. Colorado maduro wrapper is used in many of the best Honduran cigars.

Maduro is extremely dark brown, like black coffee. It is used in the kind of full-bodied cigars that experienced smokers tend to enjoy and is often associated with Cuban cigars.

Oscuro is for all intents and purposes black. It is strong, has little aroma, and is not generally used today. These wrappers typically came from Nicaragua, Brazil, Mexico, or Connecticut (but were "Broadleaf," different from Shade).

A rule of thumb is that the darker the wrapper, the stronger and deeper the cigar's taste will be. This is because the wrapper leaf's oil and sugar content are directly

Cigars come in a variety of sizes and shapes, including (from left to right) the robusto, Churchill, "bugle," torpedo, pyramides, jeroboam, and corona pictured here.

proportional to the degree of darkness. Dark wrappers contain more oil and sugar because they have been exposed to more sunlight or because they're from higher altitudes. They also have been fermented longer than lighter leaves.

SHAPE

There is nothing mysterious about the shape and size of a cigar, no special knowledge that you need. It is a matter of personal taste—and of fashion. It used to be that *torpedos* (cigars whose closed end comes to a torpedo-like point) were not popular; now they are in demand. It also used to be that American smokers preferred milder (double claro) cigars, but that fashion has changed as well. Today, Americans who have cultivated a more sophisticated smoker's palate are enjoying bigger cigars such as *robustos*, which burn more slowly, are less hot and smoky, and have a more even flavor.

All cigars are categorized as being either *parejos* (having straight sides) or *figurados* (irregular shapes). *Figurados* include the following:

ENJOY LARGER CIGARS WHEN YOU HAVE THE TIME AND SMALLER ONES WHEN YOU DON'T.

Pyramides—having a pointed, closed end (or "head") and a wider "foot."

Belicoso—a small pyramides, but with a rounded head.

Torpedo—having both ends sealed.

Culebra—three panetelas braided together, intended to be smoked individually.

SIZE

Common sense dictates that you should enjoy larger cigars when you have the time and smaller ones when you don't, but the size you choose is, again, your prerogative. Your choice should be influenced, though, by *where* you'll be smoking and *how long* you'll have to smoke. For instance, you probably won't want to light up a 9 ¼-inch Grand Corona at an intimate cocktail party. It's important that the cigar fit the setting and time frame in which it will be smoked. If you think a big cigar will give others the

The ring gauge measures the cigar's diameter in sixty-fourths of an inch.

impression that you're rich, you'll find that lighting up a big cigar in a small setting will say all that anyone needs to know about your lack of savoir faire. Rule number one for selecting a cigar is this: choose appropriately.

The cigar's girth, or diameter, is measured by a ring gauge, which measures diameter in sixty-fourths of an inch. Thus, a ring gauge of sixty-four means the cigar is one inch in diameter. Most cigars have a ring gauge between thirty and fifty-two. In general, the larger the ring gauge the more full-flavored the cigar. Their fillers contain more slow-burning *ligero* leaf, so they tend to smoke cooler and milder. They also tend to be better made because they are put together by more experienced rollers; the smaller sizes are given to newly qualified apprentice *tabaqueros*. Given a choice and sufficient time to enjoy them, connoisseurs typically prefer cigars of larger ring gauge.

Unfortunately, there are no standard sizes for the types of cigars. This means that, for example, a torpedo might be six inches long with a ring gauge of fifty, or it might be nine inches long with a ring gauge of fifty-eight. To give you an idea of the maze of choices in cigar size that will confront you, we provided a list *(page sixty-four)* of sizes of the most common cigars. They are ordered from the longest to the shortest.

Again, the shape and size of your cigar are up to you. You may want to follow the general guideline that the time of day and setting should factor into, if not altogether determine, what you smoke. For example, a milder, smaller cigar is typically smoked in the morning or after a light lunch. A robusto can provide the right ending to a heavy lunch. After a substantial dinner or late in the evening, a full-flavored Churchill or belicoso can be an excellent choice.

CRAFTSMANSHIP

The first thing to look at when judging a cigar is its wrapper. If the wrapper isn't intact, choose another cigar. It shouldn't be dry or brittle; it should be neither too hard nor too soft, and it should have a slight oiliness to the touch. It should have no large veins, but be

42

44

46

48

50

52

54

SIZE CHART

Type	Length	Ring Gauge
Grand Corona, Montecristo A	9 1/4" (235mm)	47
Torpedo, Pyramides	6–9" (152–228mm)	50–58
Double Corona	7 1/2"–8" (190–203mm)	47–52
Especial	7" (190mm)	39
Long Panetela	7" (190mm)	35–39
Churchill	7" (178mm)	46–50
Lonsdale	6 1/2" (165mm)	42–43
Corona Grande	6" (152mm)	46–48
Belicoso	5–6" (152–228mm)	50–55
Culebras	5 3/4" (145mm)	39
Corona	5"–5 3/4" (127–146mm)	42
Petit Corona	5" (127mm)	40–43
Hermoso	5" (127mm)	48
Robusto/Rotschild	4 1/2"–5" (115–127mm)	48–52
Très Petit Corona	4 1/2" (115mm)	40
Panetela	4 1/2" (114mm)	26–33
Perla	4" (102mm)	40
Demi Tasse	4" (102mm)	30–39

smooth and uniformly textured. And it should have a noticeable, pleasant bouquet. If it doesn't, it hasn't been stored properly. After you've assessed the condition and craftsmanship of the cigar, the next thing to examine is the color of the filler blend that you are able to see at the open end—also called the foot or "tuck." In general, the darker the tobacco, the greater its body and strength.

If you're buying a box of cigars, you should ask to open it first. If the salesman refuses, chances are he doesn't know what he's doing or there's something wrong with the cigars. Make sure the cigars are uniformly colored. If the color of the cigars is significantly different, you should choose another box. Smell and feel the cigars. Take the cigars between your fingers and squeeze gently from head to foot. The cigars should feel uniformly firm (not rock hard) and should not have knots, bumps, or soft spots, which would indicate hot spots or air pockets. If they make a crackling sound, they are either old or dry. If they feel mushy they haven't been stored well and will burn badly. Cigars frequently come

IF THE WRAPPER ISN'T INTACT, CHOOSE ANOTHER CIGAR.

wrapped in cellophane, which should be removed before storing them.

Also examine the cigar for little holes in the wrapper. If you see holes, chances are there is a bug inside. Tiny bugs or the eggs of bugs that attack the tobacco leaf can actually survive the fermentation and cigar-making process. Then, when conditions are right—such as inside a cozy humidor—the bug or its offspring can cut a swath of destruction through your supply of cigars. A couple of years ago, Andrew opened a newly purchased box of cigars to add them to his humidor. Upon examination, he found small holes in one of the cigars. Fearful of finding bugs inside, Andrew sliced open the cigar and found larvae. Fortunately, he made the discovery before adding the infested cigars to his humidor, where the larvae could have feasted on all his stock. Be careful!

OF NAME BRANDS AND VALUE

As you can see, there are several things to look for when determining what you want to buy and smoke. But the color, shape, size, and craftsmanship comprise the essentials of cigar knowledge. As we've said before, the pleasure from a cigar has a good deal to do with how much you know about cigars in general and about what you like in particular.

You should know, though, that brand names can be deceptive. The brand name is identified on the cigar band; for example, the names Romeo y Julieta, Partagás, H. Upmann, and Hoyo de Monterrey—are all revered Cuban cigar makers. But since Castro's revolution, many of those brands have been produced outside Cuba by Cuban expatriates. So if you are in London, say, where you can buy a wide array of Cuban cigars, you'll find Romeo y Julietas made in Cuba as well as Romeo y Julietas made in the Dominican Republic. They are completely different cigars. There will be variations between brands because of the particular blending of filler leaves as well as the country of origin. Nevertheless, cigar brands are standard, and while no two cigars are exactly alike—even from the same maker—you should notice a consistency in composition and taste.

A word about value. Spending $15 for a cigar does not guarantee you a good smoke or a taste that you'll enjoy. As we've stressed before, enjoying cigars is a matter of personal taste. If you find a cigar you like for $1.00 or $3.50, you shouldn't feel that you have to cultivate a taste for more expensive cigars

"I WAS SMOKING, AND UTTERLY HAPPY.... I DO NOT KNOW WHAT THE BRAND OF THE CIGAR WAS. IT WAS PROBABLY NOT CHOICE, OR THE PREVIOUS SMOKER WOULD NOT HAVE THROWN IT AWAY SO SOON."

—*Mark Twain*

merely to keep up with a friend who possibly knows less about cigars but spends more than you do. Your best bet is to invest a bit of time in learning about cigars and what you particularly like about them. Your investment will pay off because you'll be able to decide for yourself, based on your taste preferences and not on the ring gauge of your money wad, how much you want to spend. Remember, it is a mark of true sophistication to be able to buy what you want rather than what someone else— whether a friend or an advertiser—says you ought to have.

STORING YOUR CIGARS

Your objective in storing cigars is to maintain them in a setting where the temperature and humidity are as close as possible to the climate of the Caribbean island where they more than likely originated. The ideal climate for your cigar—and probably yourself as well—is a temperature of seventy degrees Fahrenheit with seventy percent humidity.

The interior tray of a humidor.

You shouldn't leave your newly purchased cigars out in the open for more than a couple

Aluminum tubes can extend a cigar's shelf life outside the humidor.

of hours. If they are wrapped in cellophane, don't count on the cellophane to keep the cigar properly humidified for more than a few days. Some cigars come in sealed, airtight aluminum tubes, which can preserve a cigar for longer if not subjected to drastic changes in temperature and humidity. There are a number of ways to store your cigars, ranging from the basic and inexpensive to the elaborate and expensive. How you store them will be determined by your needs and budget. The most important thing to remember is the "seventy/seventy rule": seventy degrees Fahrenheit and seventy percent humidity, the ideal temperature and humidity in which to store your cigars.

THE HUMIDOR: IDEAL STORAGE

The best way to store your cigars is in a humidor. A humidor is a hermetically sealed box, usually made of wood (the type and quality of the wood largely determines the humidor's price, which can range well into the thousands of dollars), with an element or device that holds water to keep the interior of the humidor in the ideal seventy/seventy range. Some humidors include a device called a hygrometer to monitor the internal humidity. Whatever wood the outside of the humidor is made of, the inside typically is lined in unfinished Spanish cedar, the same wood used to line cigar boxes. Oil in the Spanish cedar helps prevent the cigars from drying out and allows them to mature in storage, imbibing a light, peppery aroma from the wood.

To illustrate the difference between Spanish cedar and the American variety commonly used for cedar chests and shoe trees, let us share a personal anecdote. Andrew's father, who enjoys woodworking as a hobby, built a humidor to store his son's fine cigars. Knowing that a humidor must be lined

PERFECT STORAGE FOR CIGARS IS SEVENTY DEGREES FAHRENHEIT AND SEVENTY PERCENT HUMIDITY.

in cedar, but not understanding the difference between Pacific Northwest and Spanish cedars, Dr. Falk lined the humidor with aromatic American cedar. Although the humidor was functionally fine, even Andrew's strongest cigars took on a decidedly hamster-cage-like aroma and taste after being stored in this humidor. Not one to be discouraged easily, and willing to learn from an honest mistake, Dr. Falk tried again and succeeded, this time lining a new humidor with lighter tasting and smelling Spanish cedar. We include on page sixty-nine a picture of the second of Dr. Falk's handmade humidors.

When shopping for a humidor, you should inspect the merchandise as you would any fine piece of furniture. You want a sturdy, well-made, functional unit. Beware of any gaps in the seal of the lid, and certainly any nicks or scratches will mar the aesthetic condition of the humidor. Whatever type you decide on, be sure to keep the humidor in a cool location out of direct sunlight, to avoid drastic temperature changes. The typical humidor maintains humidity only, not temperature, so

DON'T KEEP YOUR HUMIDOR WHERE IT WILL BE PRONE TO HOT OR COLD FLASHES.

don't keep it someplace where it will be prone to hot or cold flashes. If you're willing to spend big bucks, you can get a humidor with a unit that regulates temperature as well.

TRAVELING WITH CIGARS

If you plan to take a few cigars with you to enjoy with friends, be mindful of how you transport them. Remember, cigars are fragile organic products. After they have been in humid storage, the slightest zephyr of extremely dry, cool air can quickly dry out and crack the wrappers. So you must transport them in a way that avoids shocking them— which means definitely *not* in your back pocket. There are different kinds of pocket

Carrying cases are useful when traveling with cigars.

cases you can use to carry cigars, usually made of leather or wood. A leather case should be thick enough not to bend and should also be lined to prevent the cigar from taking on a leathery scent (you don't want to smoke a cigar that tastes and smells like a horse saddle).

ALTERNATIVE STORAGE

If you don't own a humidor, you can store your cigars in the cedar box in which you bought them, but be sure to place the box inside a sealable plastic bag with a moistened sponge. Don't completely seal the bag, as it's good to have some air flow. Never allow your cigars to be exposed to direct light or to dry air. At one end of the storage spectrum, other minimal ways to store your cigars include using zip-lock bags, or a wooden box with an element to retain moisture, or even a Tupperware container—anything, really, that will maintain the seventy/seventy your cigars need. Although you will hear some say that it's okay to do so, we don't recommend that you store your cigars in the refrigerator because that will draw the moisture from them.

NEVER ALLOW YOUR CIGARS TO BE EXPOSED TO DIRECT LIGHT OR TO DRY AIR.

RESUSCITATING DRIED CIGARS

If after all your attempts to store your cigars successfully you find they have lost their moisture, don't despair. There *are* ways to revive dry cigars. One method is to place them in a partially opened box inside a plastic bag, along with a moistened sponge. It will take two to four weeks to restore them to health and you'll have to rotate the cigars every few days. If you're a regular customer of a tobacconist, feel free to ask the staff to store your box of dried cigars inside their humidor for about a month to revive them.

NOW FOR THE PLEASURE OF CIGAR SMOKING

You've learned in this chapter about colors, shapes, sizes, and a little about brands of fine cigars. And you've learned some of your options for storing them. If you think along the same lines we do, you're saying to yourself, "Okay, great. Now I want a smoke." So let's move on to talk about the few things you'll need to know once you've taken that cigar out of the humidor (or plastic bag or Tupperware), when you are savoring its visual and olfactory appeal and thinking ahead eagerly to the sensory experience you're about to enjoy. Let's turn our attention to the actual art of the smoke.

The Art of the Smoke

Just as the Cuban natives Columbus learned about included early versions of cigars in their religious rituals, so too today's aficionado sets some time apart from the hurly-burly of daily life to enjoy a good smoke. There are rituals to be observed that make cigar smoking something like a religious experience even today. Like a religious experience, a good smoke gives you the opportunity to reflect and to bestow upon yourself the gift of simply *being*. And as with any ritual, there is a fairly well-ordered sequence of doing things which, when followed correctly, can bring us into a realm of experience that we call sublime.

Scissors are one way to cut cigars.

Let's talk about the steps of the ritual you must follow. Because we cigar smokers are a discerning and inquisitive lot, we'll talk about why these steps are important, how you can easily execute them, and, most important, what they contribute to the overall pleasure of cigar smoking.

CUTTING

First things first. You must cut the closed end of the cigar to unlock the pleasures awaiting you inside that rolled tube. Don't pierce the cigar because then you'll risk turning it into nothing more than a tunnel of hot air. The

piercing implement compresses the filler leaf and impedes your drawing air through the cigar, which in turn causes overheating. You don't want your head to become a hot-air balloon fueled by overheated tobacco smoke.

Cutting with a double-bladed guillotine.

What you want instead is a clean, even cut. You could use your fingernails or teeth, which we advise against unless you have razor-edged talons or Dracula's fangs. You could use cigar scissors, which require a certain amount of skill. We suggest a guillotine. No, not the kind used during the French Revolution, just a small, handheld, portable guillotine. It can be plastic and cost a few dollars or it can be sterling and cost hundreds; it's up to you. Whatever you spend, *la guillotine* is easy to use and efficient. It will have one or two blades mounted in a simple sliding mechanism. All you do is open it, position the closed end of the cigar (just below the curve) within slicing range, and squeeze the blade(s) shut. You only want to cut off enough of the cap to expose the filler leaves and allow air to be drawn through the cigar to waft that lovely flavor into your mouth. Besides, if you cut off too much of the cap you risk having the cigar unravel, as the cap is what holds it together.

LIGHTING

Now you are ready to light up. You have a choice: lighter or match. If you decide on a lighter, don't use a fluid lighter because the fluid—like cheap charcoal

Lighting with a wooden match.

briquettes in a barbecue—will impart all manner of impurities and contaminate your cigar. Butane, on the other hand, provides a clean-burning flame and is an ideal match, as it were, for the cigar. If you don't have a butane lighter handy, ordinary wooden matches are the next best source of fire. Paper matches burn too quickly, and you'll go through several

by the time you've achieved ignition. While some romanticize the notion of tearing into strips and lighting the cedar flats from the cigar box to light the cigar, we strongly advise against the practice. The flamethrower you wind up with will blacken the cigar and possibly burn down your house.

You don't need to warm the cigar before lighting it because there are no longer gum adhesives to burn off as there used to be, a century ago. To light the cigar, place the cut end to your lips as you rotate the foot within the flame of your lighter or wooden match. Slowly turn it in the flame and draw in the smoke until it is uniformly glowing. Don't inhale, simply pucker and suck—not unlike the kiss you used to plant on your great-aunt's cheek. If it isn't burning evenly, gently blow on the lit end or relight it by holding the flame in one hand and rotating the cigar in the other.

WHAT TO LOOK FOR IN A SMOKE

One of the first things you notice about a cigar, of course, is the band around it. Bands can range from being merely the name of the

As the smoke rises, your stress level lowers.

maker to ornate portrait miniatures depicting royal personages. There are at least two theories as to why bands were first put on cigars. One is that the bands prevent the cigar's nicotine from staining the fingers. Another is that the bands provide cigar makers with a means to advertise. Whatever the reason, there is still the persistent question of whether to remove the band. The answer, as with so many of life's perplexing questions, depends on whom you ask and where you live. Ask an Englishman and he'll say that of course it is only proper to remove the band, as one doesn't wish to seem ostentatious by showing off the (presumably) renowned maker's imprint. Ask someone from the Continent, however, and your Englishman's counsel will be spurned. A general rule of thumb is to remove the band only if it slides easily off the cigar, lest by forcing it you damage the delicate wrapper.

TO REMOVE OR NOT REMOVE THE BAND ... THAT IS THE QUESTION.

You will be sorely mistaken if you think of a cigar as just a large, off-color cigarette. Don't approach a cigar as you might a cigarette, the relatively high nicotine content of which can give you a rush. You don't want to smoke one cigar after another. Besides defeating the whole sensory purpose of a cigar, chain-smoking cigars would be time-consuming and expensive. Also, cigars should never be inhaled. Again, *never*. If you do, you'll find out immediately—as John did on his birthday—why you shouldn't have.

You'll cough from the cigar's intensity and you'll probably turn green. Remember, the object is simply to savor the taste of the tobacco on the palate and the aroma in the nose. The operative word here is *savor*. There is nothing worse than a hurried cigar. A corona might take half an hour to smoke, while a larger cigar such as a Churchill could take an hour or more. Like all of life's great pleasures, a cigar is meant to be tasted, smelled, watched, and felt by the hands. Relax. Enjoy.

Bring the smoke into your mouth. Think about it. Extract the taste as you would from a fine wine. Take long rather than short puffs, but not too often. Puffing too often and too quickly will overheat the cigar and cause it to burn irregularly.

ASHES

As it burns, an ash is created. The color of the cigar's ash actually reveals the quality of the cigar and its tobacco. A white ash is considered to be superior, as it indicates that the tobacco came from better soil. A gray ash is preferable to a black ash, which signals too high a moisture content in the cigar. You don't necessarily need to tap the cigar because the ash will fall off eventually. On the other hand, you probably don't want to drop ash on your clothes or your furniture. Experience and common sense will tell you when to tap. When you tap, do it lightly.

This calls for a brief detour for a humorous story. During the famous Scopes "monkey trial," when Clarence Darrow wanted to distract the jurors from the eloquence of his opponent, William Jennings Bryan, he lit up a cigar in the courtroom (they could do that then). As the ash at the end of his cigar grew

Mark Twain sits on a New Hampshire porch in the summer of 1906, enjoying his time apart.

longer, the jurors gawked in amazement, waiting for it to drop. No one knew that Mr. Darrow had rigged his cigar with a piece of wire, run head to foot, that kept the ever-growing cylinder of ash aloft.

The ideal cigar ashtray allows you to rest the cigar between puffs in a cigar-sized groove, which of course is larger than grooves in a cigarette ashtray. As with anything having to do with cigars (or anything else, for that matter), you can spend as much as you want. Whether the ashtray is simple glass, crystal, or marble, the point is to have sufficiently large grooves to accommodate a resting cigar. A large, circular ashtray also is fine.

RELIGHTING ... AND REALIZING ENOUGH IS ENOUGH

Don't worry if your cigar goes out; they frequently do, especially when half-smoked. If it goes out, gently tap the end to remove excess ash. Blow through the cigar to discharge stale smoke, then relight it. If the cigar goes out when it's down to its last third, you may want to let it rest. Flavors in the final third tend to be more intense, which can make for a harsh, unpleasant smoke. You really don't want to end your smoke on a sour note. Another way to know it's time to end your smoke is nausea. If you smoke a cigar with no food in your stomach, you may feel light-headed. This is, logically enough, why cigars are so often enjoyed after a sumptuous meal. If, however, you're smoking on an empty stomach and feel nauseated, eat an apple. Not only will it keep the doctor away, but in our experience it will also cleanse the palate and aid in treating nicotine sickness.

WHAT'S LEFT

When you've decided the cigar's life is over, set it in the ashtray and let it expire by itself. No need to stub it out like a cigarette. As with cigarettes, though, you'll

want to clear away cigar stubs before they begin to stink up the room—which they will do quickly.

After the stubs are disposed of and your pleasant smoke is a memory, what are you left with? Well, of course there's the band—which you can collect and assemble into interesting designs—and, after a number of smokes, the box, which you can also collect. Over the years Andrew has collected cigar boxes, works of art in their own right. And, as you sample different cigars, perhaps lighting (so to speak)

on one that is particularly to your taste, you may want to keep a smoking journal. Much as wine connoisseurs keep notes on the wines they drink for future reference, you can note the qualities—good or bad—of the cigar, including the setting in which you partook of it, the occasion, and the weather. You can use the journal to compare different types of cigars, such as Dominicans with Cubans or Hondurans. This is especially helpful to keep track of brand consistency over time. If you're not interested in creating cigar-band designs, you can paste the bands in your smoking journal as a memento.

ACCOMPANIMENTS

You may wish to enhance the artfulness of your smoke by accompanying your cigar with another fine organic product, such as a single-malt Scotch, cognac, Armagnac, or port. Just as the time to enjoy these spirits is typically after a fine meal, so too a cigar is an ideal *digestif* and goes nicely with any of them. You should note, however, that the cigar and the spirit should work together, neither one over-

A fine cigar and a glass of Taylor Fladgate '77 port.

whelming the other. This is easier said than done, because like cigars, *digestifs* can be different and varied. While a certain cigar may seem an ideal match for a particular Scotch, the same cigar might be lost if it were paired with a lighter, more elegant cognac. But, as we have emphasized about cigars, you should keep in mind this is a matter of personal taste. Some people prefer a single malt with a cigar, while others will swear that a cognac is superior. In the end, the accompaniment should be determined only by what appeals to you.

A CIGAR IS AN IDEAL *DIGESTIF*.

Single-malt Scotch with a cigar: the two make a good marriage of old, traditionally made natural products derived from the bounty of the earth's specific microclimates. Single malts are produced throughout Scotland, from the Lowlands to the upper islands in the north, but the four principal single-malt regions are Islay, Skye, the Lowlands, and the Highlands (from which hail a number of the more familiar single malts). Each single malt reflects the distinct characteristics of the region in which it is made.

The peaty character and hints of caramel

pronounced in some single malts go well with the earthiness and nuttiness of cigars. Rich-tasting cigars seem to go well with single malts, which share a strong earthy character in varying degrees of intensity. Aged single malts can be more caramelly in taste and less overtly alcoholic, and a bit more elegant than their younger counterparts. A single malt from Islay seems to go best with a pungent cigar. Or you may enjoy an elegant cigar made from well-aged tobacco with an older Highland single malt, such as an eighteen-year-old Macallan's, which is aged in sherry casks to smooth out its flavor. Beware, though: drinking too strong an alcohol with a cigar may create a situation in which you are "fighting fire with fire," as the single malt and the cigar struggle to dominate your palate. The key is to balance the tastes of each so that both can be savored and appreciated.

Henry enjoys combining an elegant cigar with a brandy, preferably from Cognac or Armagnac, because neither taste then dominates. Of course there are stronger and weaker armagnacs and cognacs, but all have been distilled from grapes. These brandies have a sweetness of fruit that is lacking in a grain-based product such as whisky. The strength and warmth of the alcohol in a cognac or armagnac matches well with the power of a cigar, while the combined fruitiness and caramel notes of the spirit can offer a nice contrast with the nuttiness of a cigar. Generally speaking, cognac is more elegant and rounder on the palate than its neighbor from the south, armagnac, which can be more powerful. Both have their merits and loyal supporters. It used to be that one could buy a better bottle of armagnac for the same price as a cognac; now an armagnac from a superb producer such as Claude Darroze can fetch the same price as a great cognac. A fine Honduran cigar balances a nice VSOP or, if you are feeling prosperous, an XO cognac. Armagnacs seem to go well with a richer or heavier cigar, but a richly flavored torpedo would go nicely with Hennessy's Paradis cognac.

Ports with cigars are a classic combination. The image of a well-dressed gentleman in an exclusive club in, say, the West End of London, smoking cigars and enjoying vintage port is a staple of English novels such as Evelyn Waugh's *Brideshead Revisited* and movies such as *Chariots of Fire*. Cigars and ports both have attributes that can complement one another. The black currant fruit of a port can contrast well with the nutty, almost chocolatiness of some robust cigars. As with all

The single malt is poured and the cigars await.

accompaniments, though, one can run into trouble. Henry notes that sometimes a young, intense port filled with primary fruit flavors can obscure the subtle earthy characteristics of a cigar made from well-aged tobacco. A cigar can be overwhelmed by the high sugars in a young wine. Conversely, if you have a very old port—such as a pre-World War II port or one from a lighter vintage, the port may not be able to stand up to a very strong cigar. If the port is from such a grand house and vintage—

the legendary 1931 Nacional from Quinta do Noval, for example—the port alone may be a great treat. If you want a port with your cigar, consider one in middle development, such as a 1966 or 1970, rather than a younger 1983 or 1985.

As for coffee with a cigar, it's up to you. You may find the bitterness of coffee interferes with the taste of the cigar. On the other hand, a cup of good coffee with a light cigar in the morning or early afternoon can be exactly right.

A WORD ABOUT CIGAR DINNERS

As for cigar dinners: they are becoming increasingly popular, particularly among people newly converted to the ritualized pleasure of fine cigars. Unfortunately, though, these dinners often aren't much more than excuses for excess. Henry and Andrew attended one cigar dinner during which a different cigar was provided between each course. Neither the food nor the cigars stand out in memory. As we've tried to make clear, everything has its time and place. Smoking a cigar during the course of a meal doesn't do justice to the food, the wine, or the cigar. As the American public smokes more cigars, we hope to see more of these dinners focus on the overall dining experience, with one good cigar provided at the end of a gourmet meal.

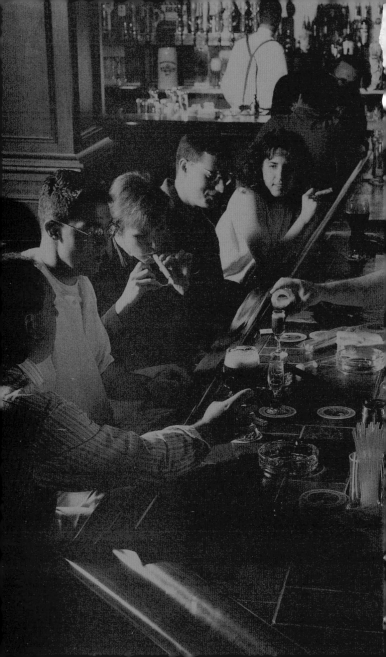

The State and Future of the Cigar Industry

The demand for high-quality cigars in the 1990s dramatically changed the cigar industry. Although the industry had been in a steady slump, during the late 1980s the interest in cigars started to heat up. Richard Carleton Hacker, author of *The Ultimate Cigar Book*, dates the resurgence of cigars' popularity to about 1989. He believes their comeback is due to a desire among middle-aged people for status symbols and leisurely pleasure. As Hacker writes, "We are all looking for a fortress where we can be free—even momentarily—from the dragons and demons we must fight. The cigar has become that fortress."

INCREASING DEMAND

The Cigar Association of America estimates that there are 10 million cigar smokers in the United States today, including several hundred thousand women. When Hacker was writing *The Ultimate Cigar Book*, only one

Cigar bars— a '90s way to share a time apart.

in ten smokers was a buyer of premium, handmade cigars—defined by the trade association as costing between $1.50 and $20.00 each. In the 1990s, though, sales of handmade cigars have soared. Americans bought 163 million premium cigars in 1995, according to the Cigar Association of America, up from 97 million just four years earlier.

Cigar "smokers" are held now throughout the country in hotels and restaurants. There is even a Cigar Line to call (800-987-0707), sponsored by Davidoff, that offers information about "cigar-friendly" establishments nationwide. When you call, a sexy English-accented female voice greets you and escorts you through the touchtone options. You can get listings of restaurants and other information, by region and event, then be connected directly to the establishment itself, or to the Davidoff shops if you want to buy some of their fine products or to say thanks for this ingenious service.

WRAPPER SHORTAGE

With the increased demand worldwide for handmade, premium cigars, there is currently a shortage of the quality dark wrapper leaf used in cigars. Besides the simple fact that less wrapper is being grown compared to fifty years ago, another reason for the shortage is that a number of areas where wrapper is produced have encountered political and economic problems at the very time that demand has increased. And in Connecticut, darker leaf is harder to grow. Connecticut Shade traditionally has been yellow or light brown in color and silky in texture. As we already noted, lighter shades of wrapper were preferred by Americans until the recent generation of more daring smokers began trying the richer, darker cigars long favored by Europeans. James Suckling reports in *Cigar Aficionado* (Spring 1995) that General Cigar is investing millions of dollars in Connecticut to increase production of the darker wrapper leaf. Cameroon and the Central African Republic have experienced enormous political upheavals that, together with a drought in 1994 that wiped out ninety-five percent of the wrapper leaf crop, have hobbled production there. Chances are good that large firms such as General Cigar, with their big wallets and large stocks of wrappers, will weather the crisis. Smaller companies without the stockpiles of wrapper leaf are likely to suffer. Remember, it may take as long as three years to process the wrapper leaf from plant to *puro*.

In Cuba, the state monopoly, Habanos, S.A. (formerly Cubatabaco) has joined the Dutch company Lippoel Leaf BV of Baarn, in a $1.2 million experiment aimed at producing Connecticut Shade wrapper for small to medium-length cigars on 500 acres in the Partidos region, about an hour west of Havana. The wrapper there is not as prestigious as that of El Corojo but it does provide a tobacco with a sweet and clean aftertaste. The future for this region's wrappers is likely to be in machine-made cigars destined for Europe. Whether the tobacco is made into cigars in Cuba or sent in bulk to be processed in the Netherlands, the benefit will lie in being higher in quality and lower in price.

THE RISKS OF OBTAINING CUBAN CIGARS IN THE UNITED STATES

Although Cuban products have been banned in the United States for more than thirty years, Americans still can obtain Cuban cigars in three ways. The only legal way to bring Cuban cigars into the country is to travel to Cuba to visit family members, to conduct academic research, or on a journalist's visa. You can then bring back up to $100 worth of Cuban products as gifts. The second way is to enjoy them while traveling abroad. Finally, there is the black market. But beware, because in addition to the risk of fines or imprisonment, the cost of Cuban cigars smuggled into the United States is exorbitant. The *New York Times* reported in April 1996 that a price list of black-market Cuban cigars seized by U.S. Customs in 1995 listed a box of fifty Coronas selling for $650—and that is $200 less than what that same box would fetch today. Besides the astronomical price, smuggled cigars are sometimes fakes. Norman Sharp, president of the Cigar Association of America, told the *Times*, "Counterfeiting Cuban cigars is a big business. All the counterfeiters have to do is say a box of cigars is Cuban and then try to rake in all these exorbitant prices. A lot of inexperienced smokers won't be able to tell the difference."

The embargo on Cuban products has produced some comical stories, too. Allow us to share a favorite. A couple of years ago, a friend who loves Cuban cigars was returning to the States from a family trip to Europe. He and his brother were carrying their personal cache of Montecristos in their backpacks. As they were passing through U.S. Customs, our friend's mother yelled to his father, "I told you not to let the boys bring the Cuban cigars through." Fortunately, the mother's

> **BESIDES THE ASTRONOMICAL PRICE, SMUGGLED CIGARS ARE SOMETIMES FAKES.**

slip of the tongue didn't result in the search and seizure it well might have. The moral of the story would seem to be that even otherwise upstanding citizens will sometimes go to great lengths to get their hands on Cuban *puros*.

CUBAN CIGAR MAKING TODAY

In Cuba today, many of the prerevolution brand names are still produced, almost exclusively for export, a fact that has raised legal concerns because of the use of the same brand names in other countries. Besides this confusion, it is not uncommon for two or more brands to be manufactured at the same factory. Because the factory happens to excel at making a particular size of cigar, it will produce that size for various brands. This is quite different from the way things were done before Castro took power. Back then, a cigar factory would either use tobacco grown on its own *vegas* or buy from one of the major tobacco brokers.

The cigar factories, or *fabricas*, in Havana now receive the finest crops to produce cigars for export. The most famous factories are the old ones such as the Real Fabrica de Tabacos Partagás and the La Corona factory, close to the capital. Other famous Cuban makers in Havana include H. Upmann, El Rey del Mundo, and Romeo y Julieta. All these were producing cigars long before Castro's takeover. One of the newer factories, created by Castro and known for the Cohiba cigars it makes, is El Laguito, set in a neoclassical villa once owned by the self-styled Marqués de Pinar del Rio, in the exclusive suburb of Miramar.

Montecristo is Cuba's most widely recognized brand, accounting for half the country's exported cigars; all the factories just mentioned produce Montecristo cigars. Even Cuba's most prized products, the Cohibas, are produced at various *fabricas*. El Laguito makes about 2 million Cohibas a year, while another one to two million are made at the old Upmann and Partagás factories. There are two reasons why production is spread out like this. One is that no one factory has the capacity to produce an entire line of cigars. The second is that rollers in different factories have become expert at making particular sizes of cigars.

Many discerning cigar smokers believe that the finest Montecristos are made at the Upmann factory, where the brand was first made by the Menendez family in the 1930s. The factory makes Montecristo No. 2s, Cohiba Esplendidos and Robustos, and Upmann's own Sir Winston Churchill. The Montecristo No. 2 is among the most difficult cigars to make; it can take a roller up to six years to perfect the art of making one. Fortunately, the Upmann factory employs the largest number of top-graded rollers of any Cuban *fabrica*. At the La Corona factory, Hoyo de Monterrey and Punch cigars are produced. At the Partagás factory cigars are made for La

Gloria Cubana, Bolivar, and Allones brands, as well as Cohiba Robustos.

An individual buying Cuban cigars can determine where and when the cigars were made by examining the box carefully. Since the mid 1980s, a two- or three-letter code has been printed in ink at the bottom of the box. Cigars made at El Laguito factory are denoted by "EL." Those made at El Rey del Mundo bear the mark "HM," H. Upmann "JM," Romeo y Julieta "BM," La Corona "FR," and Partagas "FPG." These abbreviations were assigned to the factories by Castro's government. Upmann's "JM," for example, stands for "José Marti," Cuba's nineteenth-century revolutionary hero. After the abbreviation is a letter code corresponding to the month and year of the cigars' manufacture. As we write, the code is N for 1, I for 2, V for 3, E for 4, L for 5, A for 6, C for 7, U for 8, S for 9, and O for 0. While pre-Castro cigar boxes were stamped "Made in Havana-Cuba," those made today are stamped in Spanish.

With the collapse of the Soviet Union, Cuba in the early 1990s could no longer obtain the fertilizers, string and muslin for tents, or fuel required to maintain large and high-quality tobacco production. The *Financial Times* reported in March 1996 that in 1993, Cuba's tobacco production fell to 300,000 quintales (13,800 tons), one-third of its previous harvests, while Cuba's total cigar exports were down by more than twenty-five percent, from 80 million in 1987 to a mere 57 million. A severe hurricane that struck the island in 1993 didn't help matters. The cigar slump is estimated to have cost Cuba $500 million in lost exports between 1993–1994.

A panel convened by *Cigar Aficionado* in Spring 1994 noted that if the U.S. embargo on Cuban products were lifted today and Americans were allowed to buy Cuban cigars (generally called "Havanas"), it would take several years to balance the supply and demand. In the meantime European investors are leading the charge to invest in Cuba, providing $40 million a year, according to the *Financial Times* article. The Spanish tobacco company, Tabacalera, since 1993 has invested $25 million a year in Cuba's tobacco planta-tions—supporting about half the country's tobacco-growing land. This arrangement certainly serves the Cubans well. Before planting a crop, the Cubans draw up a list of the tents, fertilizers, clothes, shoes, and other items they will need. Tabacalera goes down the list item by item, and delivers the products.

EUROPEAN INVESTORS ARE LEADING THE CHARGE TO INVEST IN CUBA.

At harvest time Habanos, S.A. determines the price that Tabacalera will pay for the tobacco, and the cost of the products is subtracted from it. In this unique financing arrangement, Tabacalera purchases more than fifty percent of all tobacco products exported from Cuba and more than half of all Cuba's handmade cigars.

In an interview with *Cigar Aficionado* (Spring 1994), Francisco Padrón, then the director of Habanos, S.A., said that although Cuba's production had fallen in 1993 after it lost sixty percent of its crop, the quality of the harvest was unaffected and in fact was very good. Padrón stated that quality has never been compromised in Cuba because Castro gave him only one rule: make cigars of the utmost quality because cigars represent Cuba to the world. Despite Padrón's reassurances, rumors abound that Cuba's large leaf-wrapper crop was decimated. Still, he claims that the country produced 200 million cigars in 1993 for the domestic market, while managing to reserve "the best" for export. During the 1995-96 growing season, observers reported

CUBA CAN PRODUCE ONLY HALF THE NUMBER OF CIGARS DEMANDED WORLDWIDE.

seeing a better quality crop in Pinar del Rio. Despite heavy rains in December and January, Cuban officials predicted the 1996 tobacco harvest would bring in 750,000 quintales (34,500 tons), an increase of 100,000 tons over 1995. However, even with maximal production, Habanos, S.A. says they can supply only half the potential worldwide market for Cuban cigars, estimated at 115 million units.

MORE ABOUT BRAND NAMES

As we noted earlier, Cuba's cigar companies were nationalized in 1960. Thousands of Cubans fled the island nation, including a number of cigar makers. Habanos, S.A., the state exporting cigar company formed by Castro, began marketing the esteemed Cuban brand names outside Cuba. Exiled cigar makers, who took their brand names with them, complained. The complicated result is that the consumer sees Cuban and non-Cuban cigars with the same name, sometimes distinguished only by the country of origin written on the wrapper or the box. Cuba lost a lawsuit in France over the ownership of the names of Montecristo and Partagás. After the court ruling, Cuba withdrew Montecristo, Partagás, and seven other brands from the French market, but replaced them with other Cuban brands, including El Rey del Mundo and Hoyo de Monterrey.

Spain's national cigar company, Tabacalera, is a major

financial backer of the Cuban cigar industry and owns a number of Cuban brand names. Beginning in the 1960s Cuba had used the trademarks for cigar brands without paying royalties on them. In the 1980s, though, the former owners of the brand names—including Montecristo, H. Upmann, Partagás, and Por Larrañaga—sued for compensation. Tabacalera negotiated with Cuban Cigar Corporation, owned by Cifuentes International and Consolidated Cigars, to purchase the trademarks. The Spanish company made a deal in 1991 to buy the Montecristo, Partagás, and other trademarks for the entire world—with the exception of Cuba, the Dominican Republic, and the United States.

Though Tabacalera obtained the trademarks, it still needed the actual cigars from Cuba. The interesting outcome of all this is that Cuba still doesn't pay a royalty to Tabacalera for the use of the name Montecristo, for example, when Habanos, S.A. sells cigars under the Montecristo label in the United Kingdom, because in the U.K., Cuba still owns the brand name of

SPAIN'S NATIONAL CIGAR COMPANY OWNS A NUMBER OF CUBAN BRAND NAMES.

Montecristo. Instead, it "pays" by supplying Tabacalera with the best tobacco leaf for its production. In the convoluted system by which Cuba sells and distributes its cigars, certain foreign entities have the right to sell particular brands or names in their countries, while in another country these rights may be given to another entity altogether.

Under the Helms-Burton Bill, recently passed in the United States, former Cuban nationals are allowed to sue in U.S. courts for property expropriated by the Castro government. The bill—signed into law by President Clinton, himself an occasional cigar smoker—requires that the Cuban national must have owned property worth at least $50,000 in 1959, the year of the Cuban revolution. If a foreign company operating in Cuba uses the property belonging to the Cuban national, the Cuban national is entitled to payment by that company. This requirement will create an extra cost for the foreign company investing capital in Cuba. Of course, the goal of the bill is to dry up foreign capital in Cuba by opening the would-be investor to potential lawsuits in U.S. courts. Perhaps not surprisingly, Adriano Martinez of Habanos, S.A., told the *Financial Times* that he didn't believe the new American law targeting foreign investors would affect the recovery of Cuba's tobacco industry.

While it remains to be seen what the impact of the Helms-Burton Bill will be, Cuba's cigar industry is moving ahead. In November 1996, Habanos, S.A. will introduce a new figurado (pointed at both ends) for sale in the English market. The small cigar, to be available in four sizes, will be called *cuaba*, after a word by Cuba's Taino Indians to denote a local species of quick-burning bushes. Habanos, S.A.'s Adriano Martinez says the state cigar company is training a group of expert rollers to make these new cigars. Habanos, S.A. believes this type of cigar—which was popular in the nineteenth century—will be received by smokers as a novelty and a welcome contrast to the large Churchill sizes that have been so popular.

LOOKING AHEAD

Where will the explosion of interest in fine cigars go? Of course, no one can say for sure. It's likely the increased demand will lead to greater investment in the cigar industries in countries such as the Dominican Republic and Honduras, to enable them to produce more. Another possibility is that the demand for high-quality cigars might lead to the

IT'S LIKELY THAT INCREASED DEMAND WILL LEAD TO GREATER INVESTMENT IN THE CIGAR INDUSTRIES IN THE DOMINICAN REPUBLIC AND HONDURAS.

establishment of smaller, boutique-type cigar makers—
similar to the rash of microbreweries making specialty beers.
We can only hope that the revival of what had been a declin-
ing industry doesn't lead to an onslaught of mercenaries
offering fancy prices for not-so-well-made products. As we
have stressed, value is important in determining whether a
cigar is worth buying and smoking.

All these are certainly issues worthy of consideration.
But the problems won't be solved overnight and the future
is unforeseeable. So for now, let's just kick back, light up,
and do nothing more than appreciate and enjoy the art of
fine cigars.